66 Kilos of Solitude

Ardita Jatru

Transcendent Zero Press

Houston, Texas

Copyright © 2018 Ardita Jatru.

PUBLISHED BY TRANSCENDENT ZERO PRESS
www.transcendentzeropress.org

All rights reserved. No part or parts of this book may be reproduced in any format whether electronic or in print except as brief portions used in reviews, without the expressed written consent of Transcendent Zero Press, or of the author Ardita Jatru.

ISBN-13: 978-1-946460-01-1

Printed in the United States of America

Transcendent Zero Press
16429 El Camino Real Apt. 7
Houston, TX 77062

Cover design by Glynn Monroe Irby

Cover image taken from http://wzory-tatuazy.com/galeria-zdjec/tatuaz-rozy,i33.html

66 Kilos of Solitude

Ardita Jatru

66 Kg (150 pound) of Solitude – Review on a book not found in bookstores!

(Arlinda Guma is the author of two novels and several columns in Tirana's press)

I read the poetry of Ardita Jatrù ten years ago on the Internet.

A *par excellence* poem, which, among other things, is permeated by a fragile, beautiful, blubber.

Artistically perfect, fluid, with a clear sincerity and a warm mix of aromas of Albania, where the poet was born, and the city of Thessaloniki, where she has lived for many years.

I cannot give a nationality to this poem, but I can call it quite well a European poetry; because it is completely out of the schematic restrictions that have left in the unconscious of the Albanian authors (even the young ones) the socialist realism.

There is a lot of soul in Ardita's poetry, as there is a prominent hood, unlike anybody else. While I often find myself reading speech games poetry, that leave nothing to the mind, the beauty of Ardita's poetry lies in the fable, each poem has a prominent fable that is easily remembered.

Ardita is capable to transform in poetry the least possible poetic thing.

Ardita Jatrù is distinguished for the delicate sensitivity, but some of her other poems are the opposite of this delicacy. They are almost whipping and neatly brutal, truly brutal.

One day I asked Ardita where I could find her book of poetry and she replied: "Please do not hurt me! I keep the books in closet and give them to friends."

I was saddened. I did not want to hurt her, but with delicacy I continued to say that I wanted to buy the book and I did not like it as a gift, because I consider it as a sign of respect for the work of the artist. But I did not know where to buy it because, what is most regrettable, Ardita's books are not found in the bookstores of Albania. And this not because they are sold out, but because they do not exist in bookstores. They never existed; they do not know how to stay in bookstores. The only thing they know is to lie down in the "closet".

Indeed, it is often the case that good books are not found in Albanian bookstores, while the readers look for books of media characters that are distinguished for their "encyclopedic ignorance". (Remind you here how much I have been tired of finding a poetry book by the great poet, Frederick Rreshpja.)

I ask Ardita why her books are not found in bookstores, and she tells me that after contacting some publishers and she did not receive an answer ("My name didn't "show" anything to them", she said, even though Ardita was published in several literary magazines, Greek, English, etc.) she finally found a publisher who said: "No one reads poetry".

The last sentence reminded me of a bookkeeper in Tirana, one day I asked for a book poem by Alain Bosquet, and he said: "You still looking for something lost, no one reads poetry today."

So I'm writing this promotional article for Ardita's poetry, while the reader can't find the book.

And I mean a poem like this:

> Ana,
> take care of me,
> please brush my hair by your thin fingers
> because for you I've created a canticle.
> Come on, sponge me down for the last time
> and forgive me darling as you forgive the rain
> when it overturns the leaves on the ground, unwittingly.
> Inside the drawer there is a Music Sheet,
> open it to the last page and sing it without sound.
> Receive it as a gift,
> and then tell me,
> if it lacks something to be perfect.
> Ana,
> an apple is waiting to be peeled. Peel it!
> In the vase, the flower is eager for some water. Water it!

Albanians do not love poetry? Isn't this a hasty assertion?
In Albania and in all the former communist countries, there are more poets than novelists.

Albanians have a good tradition of poetry. Dictatorships have been careful with poetry; because of ideology they have given it an important place.

The problem lies precisely in the area of publishers. Getting a license to open a publishing house is not just a business matter. When opening a publishing house, publishers have a moral responsibility to the nation about what food they will serve. The publisher guides general tastes. Literature is the backbone of a nation; all the arts derive from it; without a beautiful literary text we cannot create a good song and without a good script, from "the hand" of a writer, we cannot create a good movie. And leaving it in hands that are directed only to profitability rather than quality is one of the biggest crimes someone can do to a nation.

Albanian publishers do not try to promote poetry like this; "that goes to the core"... (Borrowing one of Ardita's verses)

> There were times I wanted to strangle you.
> That evening, that whore with naked chest
> in front of me trying to seduce and having her eyes on you
> I wanted to strangle her too,
> but I restrained myself,
> then I have held to no purpose your fingers
> that we have interweaved
> and then I looked myself in the mirror
> inside of which you have been entered
> and in front of it I felt, my God, so frightful.
> But I have tried to control myself again.
> That night, I was a wolf in bed
> and we climaxed in full flower
> and then you slept peacefully.
> I waited a bit and I lit a cigarette on the balcony
> then a second one,
> a third .... that beautiful whore
> who had her eyes on you, appeared in front of me
> and made my blood ran cold

After many tries and troubles, Ardita published her book in a printing house.

It is sad and painful that such poems are not found in bookstores:

> My mother had only one dress,
> she washed it at night and dried it near the cooker.
> She put it on next day with a new flavor.
> I never asked her why she didn't buy a second one.
> I didn't want her to have a second one.
> I knew her in that way
> in long dress to her knees
> with pink flowers.
> When she bought a yellow silk shirt
> I cut it into pieces at night by scissors
> and filled my pockets.
> Mommy hushed two days
> and I rejoiced inside of me

> that she wore again the same dress,
> and I repeated to myself,
> how I want to look like her.
> Now I began to understand my mother.
> I solved the yesterday questions.

It's sad, painful, that schoolchildren know most of the poets of the dictatorship.

It's sad, painful, that post-90's poets like Ardita are not included in the textbooks.

It is disappointing how the Ministry of Culture grants funds to its militant supporters to translate their works into other languages, while the works of truly talented authors such as Ardita are not even in the bookstore.

An almost hostile indifference.

And this indifference increases when the author is a woman.

I invite you to read the poems of Ardita Jatrù. If you do not read it, it is not the author that loses but the reader does. Meanwhile, drummers on the mediocre works of "universal nothingmakers" will continue to fall, announcing the funeral of literature.

It seems that with the title of 66 kg (150 pound) of solitude, Ardita Jatrù anticipated painfully the difficult path of her book. Because that is the great solitude of Albanian emigrants, gifted like Ardita, for whom the state has no care. Talents without homeland. Couple of souls lost on a strap of land that the motherland never fed them...

Published in "Gazetën Shqiptarja.com" August 6th, 2017

TABLE OF CONTENTS

My passing / 11

Last song / 12

Whores of my city / 13

Go to sleep my darling / 14

My Father-land / 15

I'm going to sleep / 16

It came a day / 17

Sometimes I wanted to strangle you / 18

25 * / 19-20

The dress / 20

Dezi / 21

One day we will get on the train / 22

Everything will remain here / 22

The most vilified woman in our neighborhood / 23

You run away / 24

People who didn't love me / 25

Does hell let in a loser? / 25

The nights that bed doesn't fit me in / 26

Your shoes / 27

Hesitancy / 28

My passing

Twenty-five years of my passing,
I took away with me what I could,
what I couldn't take I left behind.
Chamomile field wasn't handpicked by anyone else
and some mimosa trees in Students' City remained without grasping.
(In March, I used to prepare the most beautiful bouquets)
There was left behind that little child with blond hair
at the door holding that paperboard:
Mihal Grameno Street, No. 6.
God's hand remained in the air
and two eyes looking at the back through the bursts of tears.
All of those were taken away by the river.
I did not even have time to cry.
Twenty-five years of my passing,
what I took away with me
I am keeping it on the palm of my hand
by eating my heart out.
What I left behind
was a girl who became a woman.

Last song

Ana,
take care of me,
please brush my hair by your thin fingers
because for you I've created a canticle.
Come on, sponge me down for the last time
and forgive me darling as you forgive the rain
when it overturns the leaves on the ground, unwittingly.
Inside the drawer there is a Music Sheet,
open it to the last page and sing it without sound.
Receive it as a gift,
and then tell me,
if it lacks something to be perfect.
Ana,
an apple is waiting to be peeled. Peel it!
In the vase, the flower is eager for some water. Water it!
White scarf, which isn't put on for two winters, put it on you!
And now, open the window darling
to enjoy the melody of the forest
as it is getting in the nude this season.
Oh, inside my head there is just silence.
Do you feel the trembling of air?
It's the breath of God.
Your face is his imagery!
I was lost without you, Ana,
mooncalf as a blind, miserable as a deaf.
Ana,
the dog is whining,
it warns the pilgrimage of the soul.
What is beyond the forest, Ana...?

Whores of my city

The whores of my city
were beautiful girls,
incoming queens from antiquity.
Berraka had its queen,
Semiramis, the courtesan of Babylon.
At the "Tomb of Bam" Helena was leading
and the Trojans were guarding her by night and day.
Each neighborhood had a queen
and its whore had to be beautiful.
When they were moving forward on the boulevard,
O Lord, how absolutely free they were!
From behind their backs some hisses or stones.
The boulevards boys
suddenly turned into fighters.
I was a kid when the whores reigned
and one day I heard at the door the ladies of my neighborhood
when Mereme burst into sighs:
Ladies, you should have the whores' good luck,
because for us honest women
no man has killed himself.

.

Go to sleep my darling

Go to sleep my darling
because I will come near you.
We spent all our life in one bed
and the whole life is wasted.
Debts and sleep.
Go to sleep my darling.
I will come to join your breath
and both to wrap nicely the pipes with sheets
for not feeling cold
because we have nothing else to do.
Perhaps,
God has a fancy for making us birds
or maybe squirrels
in the Second Life.
Who knows!
Let's see and believe.
Let's go to sleep, darling,
in our quiet bed.
We won at least something as inheritors,
but we lost our mind.
Who cares?
Everything that we have done we did it with full breathing.
We asked no one
and happen that we owe to everyone.
Good night.
We slept.
There is some other part
to be wasted.

My Father-land

You never invited me to the wedding parties.
You did the wedding parties of too many sons.
You didn't invite me in your birthday either
and you didn't think to give me some dessert
because was all taken inside the buckets
and was eaten and bitten by hungry sons
that you keep inside your bosom.
I didn't complain again.
Nor for the death you never think to call me.
I am the latest one to know
when the face of dead son is covered with soil
and I didn't complain again.
My Father-land has trouble, I say,
because his sons remained in cross- country roads
and he didn't knows yet their children
and the Father-land has a small house
which doesn't fit in all of us.
Other sons work in remote places
to built a new big house
hoping that one day their wish become true.
The Father- land has headache, I say.
It's not his fault.
And I always feel to visit him suddenly
in wicked time
when my Father -land is very busy
and doesn't have time to talk to me.
And didn't complain again
because an adult justifies his parents
in that day when he realizes
that Father- land wasn't a god.

I'm going to sleep

I'm going to sleep.
Some peace, please.
I need to sense how the night breathes
and my soul slips along the stairs
and my body becomes snippy
and my knocked to pieces body I put in the bed.
Then I cover my body with two meters sighs.
Poor tired me,
is gone even this day and didn't says something to you.
Is gone without a beautiful voice like a joke.
I beg you for some peace, please.
I go to sleep,
because tomorrow unwillingly
I will again run up against the gods.

It came a day

It came a day, when
we were told the greatest lie
we ate it with bread
and went to sleep hungry.
We created also a God
and my mother sold her blood,
three hundred grams a month for three bucks
and her morning kiss smelled lead
with the bottle of milk in her purse.
My young mother, anemic, looked old,
my father in prison,
my brothers grew up prematurely.
And then another day came
when we trampled underfoot our god with full enmity.
The court poets burned their poems.
Then we escaped without seeing the path
into the crossroad wondering,
we, the poor of the world.
It came today
when is sprouted the same old seed
and the seed became a sapling
and the sapling became a tree with strong roots.
From a point of earth
I'm following the way back across the sky.
By paper airplanes I'm sending to my mother my greetings.

Sometimes I wanted to strangle you

There were times I wanted to strangle you.
That evening, that whore with naked chest
in front of me trying to seduce and having her eyes on you
I wanted to strangle her too,
but I restrained myself,
then I have held to no purpose your fingers
that we have interweaved
and then I looked myself in the mirror
inside of which you have been entered
and in front of it I felt, my God, so frightful.
But I have tried to control myself again.
That night, I was a wolf in bed
and we climaxed in full flower
and then you slept peacefully.
I waited a bit and I lit a cigarette on the balcony
then a second one,
a third .... that beautiful whore
who had her eyes on you, appeared in front of me
and made my blood ran cold
and in that moment I wanted to put my hands in your throat
to strangle you asleep
but the next day we said "Good morning".
We kissed.
Did you sleep well, my darling?
Peacefully, I said: And you?
And secretly I laugh at myself
how often I wanted to strangle you.

25 *

I left
and by my eyes I measured the way to the sky
because there I had to go
 and I went with noise without knowing the path that leads over there.
I walked and I have found myself in front of a church
and I went inside.
There were just me and the priest
and some lit candles for wishes, prayers
and souls of the dead.
I sat in a corner
and saw the dome of the church that was ascending
and getting up until was open, became a celestial hole
and then the rain fell on me and I thought of you.
And I was back again.
I opened the door
and we were unable to say a word
but we were drowned into kisses till to nails' hooks
and you held me tight in your chest
then we both cried
and with a voice as were from the bottom of the sea
 I said to you: I don't want to go anymore!
And we were wrapped up by our shell, we closed it up
and we remembered the beautiful things
and the tomorrow weather, we thought, what color would have had.

You have gone silently
You always do your things silently
I am the confusion.
You've closed the door slightly behind
and what happened to you then I do not know
but I know about myself, that I was hidden inside of cigarettes' smoke
until you came back again.
You appeared at the door as good breaking news
in the midst of mourning.
You had dissipated the smoke by your breath
and the same thing happened again.
We were drowned into kisses,
you held me tight in your chest till to an "oh"
and we dangled on our arms as much as we were exhausted
then we laughed it up with ourselves as it was all a joke
and suddenly you got a serious look
and in a watery look as a delicate baby you said:
I don't want to go away from you!

Until one day neither of us had guts to escape.
We changed the lock.
We set the key.
We weren't young anymore.

The Dress

My mother had only one dress,
she washed it at night and dried it near the cooker.
She put it on next day with a new flavor.
I never asked her why she didn't buy a second one.
I didn't want her to have a second one.
I knew her in that way
in long dress to her knees
with pink flowers.
When she bought a yellow silk shirt
I cut it into pieces at night by scissors
and filled my pockets.
Mommy hushed two days
and I rejoiced inside of me
that she wore again the same dress,
and I repeated to myself,
 how I want to look like her.
Now I began to understand my mother.
I solved the yesterday questions.
From out sighs I began to understand
just why she overstrained,
why she fought alone.
After all, why she should have only a dress?
For all this, I understand one thing,
that I am growing up and I am like her
but in different dresses.
I fight together with someone else
and my seasons are getting gray in the mirror.

Dezi

For the first time I got drunk off
of one glass of screw driver at Crystal Café.
It was served to me by Dezi, the buxom waitress
who was talking and hinting jokes with dirty words.
She was marvelous.
You're not from here; she told me that night,
so I treat you girl with another glass.
I drunk the first glass to the health of my boyfriend,
the second to the health of Dezi,
the third ... I got lost.
And ward boys stood on the steps of Crystal Café.
They were, with freak nicknames
Boulevard boys
who lured high school girls
and marvelous Dezi,
who was shaking her hips when walking in and out
with confidence
that the boys will enter in to drink some screw driver.

Dezi doesn't serve over there anymore,
Is neither Crystal Café nor nicknamed boys
who longed for Dezi
(I longed for her too)
But they left some laughs to the stairs
and some inebriation by screw driver.
If you see the buxom waitress in the town
sent to her the greetings from the girl
who wasn't from that county
(of course she did not remember me)
and say to her,
I intend to make an application to mayor
to put up a statue
dedicated to marvelous Dezi
who served love drinks
talking and hinting jokes with dirty words,
there, on the groundsel
of the former Crystal Café,
with tray in hand,
forever
as my first insobriety.

One day we will get on the train

One day
we will get on the train
We will sit silently inside windows
in drawn faces and aging bodies
without shoulders
and will wait whistle arrival at the station a
nd then detrain out of sight
and move to a place with soft soil
we will find a small house as a body
and lie down
and our heads throughout on a pillow of stone,
with empty pockets.
At that moment will fly over the open roof
a flock of dreams in colors that we did not apprehend.
We will lengthen our eyesight,
but we will feel like a weak plant
with curved body
that is ready to be surrender to the land.

Everything will remain here

Everything will remain here
the breach Pomegranate on the ledge
and the purple sunset
of loveless Sunday,
the sandals with broken heels
and then my stupor.

Here will remain
the two dishes on the table
and the repasts in silence
as the last straw of the joy.
Some hairs in my comb
and my tired face in the mirror.

A gale blew
And you didn't feel either the door
which was closed behind you.

The most vilified woman in our neighborhood

The most vilified woman in our neighborhood was Eli.
She was raised in an orphanage.
We all knew, but we hadn't seen
Eli circulating nude at home
without panties at all,
shameless,
and ward boys guarded every evening
on the terrace of the opposite block
to see Eli without her panties through windows
with that beautiful thing bared
and her jutted out breasts as fresh apples.
One day, someone had written on her door,
"Eli, I want to fuck you"
There yelled Camille, Lilly and Jia.
They took rags, swept off and scoured Eli's door
Shameful, what the kids would read.
O Lord, what woman they had in their palace
and they closed within a few hours their husbands.
And there was a day
that Eli went abroad forever
and there sprung a great tranquility.
Finally, the mothers of boys got rid of her
The whore went away, they said, that's it.
On the terrace of the opposite block
remained some small footprints
and boyish craving waiting for Eli
to appear naked as before
with that beautiful and bared thing.

You run away

You run away
and take everything with you.
All my beauties go up after you
and leave me a blob of breath
and some cloudlets on my head gloomily
some ethereal naps in midday
that break me off and I can't hold myself on.
I have three sleepless nights.
You run away and I presume everything
how many steps away are you now
from the front door
and what weather is expecting you there.
I curse myself to be eyeless
because I had my eye on you
then it destroyed your peace
under the mess that I have inside of my head.

People who didn't love me

Yesterday I raised over the roof a white flag.
I'm in peace with you
that for a reason you didn't love me
and now I love you more.
You came to me coated with masks
and in front of me you have been naked,
like little kids
and I saw you in tight squeeze as far as a hand
you cried a river with resounding,
and I kept your pain on the palm of my hand.
You fled coated again with masks
and I never betrayed you.
O slaves,
who unwittingly professed me about human nature!
Now you are even with me,
You damned hypocrites!
I didn't love my loneliness so much before.

Does Hell let in a loser?

My eyes establish distances,
My heart trembles
and sometimes is broken ...

Woman,
you're halfway, said to me the tailor
and points to the meter.
Without eyes and feet you cannot go to death
and I ask him,
Does Hell let in a loser?

The nights that bed doesn't fit me in

There are some nights
that bed doesn't fit me in,
some sleepless nights with heavy cushions,
some headachy nights by my thoughts
and I stare at one ceiling point
and I vent.
Then I stand up like crazy,
I go upstairs
onto the roof.
What universal peace!
So,
here I feel a wise god of loneliness.
Near the morning
I go downstairs carefully,
barefoot
with folded arms
and I go in bed by holding my breath
because I don't want to wake you up
I turn off the lights of the eyes,
close the mouth's doors
and sleep
and I don't let you know
where I've been all night
sometimes when the bed didn't fit me in.

Your shoes

You always leave your shoes
on the threshold of the door.
You come and take them off there,
put them on and run away.
So fast are your escapes and returns
with your light shoes on the edge of the door
all emit stars of sand, filled with oxygen.
There are no shoes since last two days
on the threshold of the door.
You took them, put them on and ran away.
Now I have nothing to cry for.
At least you should ran away barefoot.
You took away from me even the shoes.

Hesitancy

She brings near his hand over her lips
and kiss it easier
then gently puts his right hand on her breast
where is heaving a half of breath.
Then bursts out sobbing as hailstorm
and from the two peaks of shoulders' bones
are jumping quickly in the air some crystal particles
in the form of a complaint
then he looks at me by the two turbulent pools
which are merging at the point of the chin
and he is asking: Is there a god?
Yes it's.
But why then God took Tula in?
Her heart has failure.
Jordan is bedridden, why God doesn't take him in?
His heart is strong.
If so it is unfair,
it is terrible,
well here why is no heart,
this part here though why is empty,
why should this side of the chest was empty
how can be held the soul in a handful heart?
Please Lord,
do a hefty job.
To this cross of skeleton
you take away its soul,
you take away its soul
quickly...

*

It's nine o'clock p.m. of winter.
Beside her is lying the senescent faith.
Jordan's soul slips
from the left to the right
then in reverse.
She is crying
I am wiping her tears.
She is waiting wandering
while I read to her the Bible.
It's eleven o'clock p.m. of winter.

ABOUT THE POET

Ardita Jatru was born in 1972 in Tiranë, Albania. Her passions include photography, writing, traveling, and time with family and friends. Her poems have been published in these international magazines: Knot Magazine (USA), Section 8 Magazine (USA), Dead Snakes (CANADA), Madison Lake & Erotic Anthology Poetry (USA), 1947 Literary Journal (USA), The Tower (UK) and Duane's PoeTree (USA). Her poems are also published in Poetix (Greece), Poiein (Greece), Maison de la Poesie Anthology (Belgium), Le capital des most (France), Haemus Review (Romania) and Les Folies- Erotique (France). She lives with her husband and two daughters in Thessaloniki, Greece.

ABOUT THE TRANSLATOR

Laureta Petoshati is an Albanian poet, prose writer and translator. She was born in Vlora, Albania where still lives recently. After graduating from Industrial High School, Laureta Petoshati attended Faculty of Engineering in University of Tirana for about five years and received a Master Degree in Civil Engineering (Water Engineering) in 1987. She quit her work as water engineer in 1991, and a few years later she got the Master Degree to begin a career as a freelance translator and writer and from that time on she committed to translations, literature and journalism. She published her first poetry collection *Goddess of Heaven* in 1996, as well her historical novel *Return to Ventotene* in 2012. In 2016 she translated the 2/3 of the poetry volume *"The Temple of Loneliness"* by well-known Israeli poet Zvika Szterfeld from English into Albanian. She worked as a journalist in several newspapers and reporter in Vlora Channel Television mainly in her hometown Vlora. She continues to publish her poetry cycles and essays in many national and international newspapers such Nacional, Ndryshe, Albanian American newspaper - "Illyria" in New York, Knot Magazine, WritingRawPoetry (USA), Tuck Magazine, etc. As a poet she is a winner of one poetry contest which took place in her hometown, she won the Third Prize at the National Poetry Word Contest for 2017 in Tirana Albania, Special Prize
   The literary-scientific work of the Albanological Institute of Pristina' at the International Poetry Festival organized by the Association of Writers of Kosovo in June 2017 and as a translator she is a Winner of the first place in poetical translations at the national competition dedicated to the 75th birth anniversary of writer Dritwro Agolli and The Pegasian Alternative Academy announced her The best translator for 2016, etc. The poems translated by Laureta Petoshati from Italian and English into Albanian written by world well-known poets have been published and are still publishing in the Albanian Newspaper Nacional while the poems translated by her from Albanian into English written by some prominent Albanian poets have been published in magazines such as: Section&Magazine (USA), WritingRawPoetry (USA), The Dallas Review (USA), Safe Harbor, Of/with: journal of immanent renditions(USA), Travel Poetics, International Journal of Travel Writing, (USA), HARBINGER ASYLUM, (USA), Duane's

PoeTree (USA), Dead Snakes magazine(Canada),THE POETRY SHED in UK, The Seventh Quarry magazine Wales, (UK), PEEKING CAT POETRY MAGAZINE (UK), OPA -Anthology of CONTEMPORARY WOMEN'S POETRY 2017, etc.

www.ingramcontent.com/pod-product-compliance
Lightning Source LLC
Chambersburg PA
CBHW031440040426
42444CB00006B/902